1940 U.K.

YEARBOOK

ISBN: 9781090221810

This book gives a fascinating and informative insight into life in the United Kingdom in 1940. It includes everything from the most popular music of the year to the cost of a buying a new house. Additionally, there are chapters covering people in high office, the best-selling films of the year and all the main news and events. Want to know which team won the Football League War Cup or which British personalities were born in 1940? All this and much more awaits you within.

INDEX

FIRST EDITION

1940

January
M	T	W	T	F	S	S
1	2	3	4	5	6	7
8	9	10	11	12	13	14
15	16	17	18	19	20	21
22	23	24	25	26	27	28
29	30	31				

◐:2 ●:9 ◑:17 ○:24 ◐:31

February
M	T	W	T	F	S	S
			1	2	3	4
5	6	7	8	9	10	11
12	13	14	15	16	17	18
19	20	21	22	23	24	25
26	27	28	29			

●:8 ◑:16 ○:23

March
M	T	W	T	F	S	S
				1	2	3
4	5	6	7	8	9	10
11	12	13	14	15	16	17
18	19	20	21	22	23	24
25	26	27	28	29	30	31

◐:1 ●:9 ◑:17 ○:23 ◐:30

April
M	T	W	T	F	S	S
1	2	3	4	5	6	7
8	9	10	11	12	13	14
15	16	17	18	19	20	21
22	23	24	25	26	27	28
29	30					

●:7 ◑:15 ○:22 ◐:29

May
M	T	W	T	F	S	S
		1	2	3	4	5
6	7	8	9	10	11	12
13	14	15	16	17	18	19
20	21	22	23	24	25	26
27	28	29	30	31		

●:7 ◑:14 ○:21 ◐:29

June
M	T	W	T	F	S	S
					1	2
3	4	5	6	7	8	9
10	11	12	13	14	15	16
17	18	19	20	21	22	23
24	25	26	27	28	29	30

●:6 ◑:13 ○:20 ◐:27

July
M	T	W	T	F	S	S
1	2	3	4	5	6	7
8	9	10	11	12	13	14
15	16	17	18	19	20	21
22	23	24	25	26	27	28
29	30	31				

●:5 ◑:12 ○:19 ◐:27

August
M	T	W	T	F	S	S
			1	2	3	4
5	6	7	8	9	10	11
12	13	14	15	16	17	18
19	20	21	22	23	24	25
26	27	28	29	30	31	

●:3 ◑:10 ○:18 ◐:26

September
M	T	W	T	F	S	S
						1
2	3	4	5	6	7	8
9	10	11	12	13	14	15
16	17	18	19	20	21	22
23	24	25	26	27	28	29
30						

●:2 ◑:8 ○:16 ◐:24

October
M	T	W	T	F	S	S
	1	2	3	4	5	6
7	8	9	10	11	12	13
14	15	16	17	18	19	20
21	22	23	24	25	26	27
28	29	30	31			

●:1 ◑:8 ○:16 ◐:24 ●:30

November
M	T	W	T	F	S	S
				1	2	3
4	5	6	7	8	9	10
11	12	13	14	15	16	17
18	19	20	21	22	23	24
25	26	27	28	29	30	

◑:6 ○:15 ◐:22 ●:29

December
M	T	W	T	F	S	S
						1
2	3	4	5	6	7	8
9	10	11	12	13	14	15
16	17	18	19	20	21	22
23	24	25	26	27	28	29
30	31					

◑:6 ○:14 ◐:22 ●:28

PEOPLE IN HIGH OFFICE

Monarch - King George VI

Reign: 11th December 1936 - 6th February 1952
Predecessor: Edward VIII
Successor: Elizabeth II

Prime Minister

Neville Chamberlain - Conservative
28th May 1937 - 10th May 1940

Winston Churchill - Conservative
10th May 1940 - 26th July 1945

Ireland

Canada

United States

Taoiseach Of Ireland
Éamon de Valera
Fianna Fáil
29th December 1937
- 18th February 1948

Prime Minister
Mackenzie King
Liberal Party
23rd October 1935
- 15th November 1948

President
Franklin D. Roosevelt
Democratic Party
4th March 1933
- 12th April 1945

Australia

Prime Minister
Robert Menzies (1939-1941)

Brazil

President
Getúlio Vargas (1930-1945)

China

Premier
Chiang Kai-shek (1939-1945)

Cuba

President
Federico Laredo Brú (1936-1940)
Fulgencio Batista (1940-1944)

Egypt

Prime Minister
Aly Maher Pasha (1939-1940)
Hassan Sabry Pasha (1940)
Hussein Sirri Pasha (1940-1942)

France

President
Albert François Lebrun (1932-1940)
Vacant (1940-1944)

Germany

Chancellor
Adolf Hitler (1933-1945)

India

Viceroy of India
Victor Alexander John Hope (1936-1943)

Italy

Prime Minister
Benito Mussolini (1922-1943)

Japan

Prime Minister
Nobuyuki Abe (1939-1940)
Mitsumasa Yonai (1940)
Fumimaro Konoe (1940-1941)

Mexico

President
Lázaro Cárdenas (1934-1940)
Manuel Ávila Camacho (1940-1946)

New Zealand

Prime Minister
Michael Joseph Savage (1935-1940)
Peter Fraser (1940-1949)

Russia

Communist Party Leader
Joseph Stalin (1922-1952)

South Africa

Prime Minister
Jan Smuts (1939-1948)

Spain

Prime Minister
Francisco Franco (1938-1973)

Turkey

Prime Minister
Refik Saydam (1939-1942)

BRITISH NEWS & EVENTS

JAN

1st	Britain calls up 2,000,000 nineteen to twenty-seven-year olds for military service.
3rd	Unity Mitford, daughter of David Freeman-Mitford, 2nd Baron Redesdale, and fervent admirer of Adolf Hitler, having attempted suicide, returns to England from Germany (via Switzerland); she is carried down the gangplank of the cross-channel ferry at Folkestone on a stretcher.
5th	Oliver Stanley replaces Leslie Hore-Belisha as Secretary of State for War; Hore-Belisha had been sacked after falling out with the leading officers.
8th	Food rationing is introduced for bacon, butter and sugar. Successive ration schemes follow for meat, tea, jam, biscuits, breakfast cereals, cheese, eggs, lard, milk, and canned and dried fruit.

9th January - The 10,000-ton passenger liner Dunbar Castle of the Union Castle Line hits a mine in the English Channel and sinks with the loss of 9 men, including the Captain, Henry Atherton Causton. The 189 survivors are rescued by the minesweeper HMS Calvi and a coastal barge, and taken to the Kent coast. Chief Officer Robinson was later awarded an OBE for his part in the evacuation of the survivors from the ship.

17th	A wave of freezing weather afflicting most of Europe leads to the River Thames freezing for the first time since 1880. *Fun fact: January 1940 becomes the coldest month of any kind since February 1895, and the second coldest January of the 20th century (after 1963).*
18th	An explosion at Waltham Abbey Royal Gunpowder Mills kills five and breaks windows as far away as the East End of London. *Interesting fact: For over 300 years the Royal Gunpowder Mills were one of the most important sites in the world for the development of explosives - it closed in 1991.*

FEB

3rd — The first enemy aircraft of WWII is shot down near Whitby, North Yorkshire. The German Heinkel He 111 bomber, on a mission to attack shipping off the North East coast of Britain, was intercepted by Hawker Hurricane fighters from No.43 Squadron based at RAF Acklington.

16th — Altmark Incident: Royal Navy destroyer HMS Cossack (F03) pursues German tanker Altmark into the neutral waters of Jøssingfjord in southwestern Norway and frees the 299 British seamen held aboard.

MAR

Frisch-Peierls memorandum: Otto Frisch and Rudolf Peierls, at this time working at the University of Birmingham, calculate that an atomic bomb could be produced using very much less enriched uranium than had previously been supposed, making it a practical proposition. It helped send both Britain and America down a path which led to the MAUD Committee, the Tube Alloys project, the Manhattan Project, and ultimately the atomic bombings of Hiroshima and Nagasaki.

3-9th — The 83,673-ton RMS Queen Elizabeth makes her secret maiden voyage from Clydebank to New York. Captain John Townley zigzagged across the Atlantic to elude German U-Boats, taking six days at an average speed of 26 knots. After his arrival in New York Captain Townley received two telegrams, one from his wife congratulating him and the other from Her Majesty Queen Elizabeth thanking him for the vessel's safe delivery. *Interesting facts: During her WWII service as a troopship RMS Queen Elizabeth carried more than 750,000 troops and sailed some 500,000 miles.*

16th — Twenty-seven-year-old James Isbister becomes the first WWII civilian casualty of a bombing in the UK. He died after a Junkers Ju 88, returning from a raid on the naval base of Scapa Flow, jettisoned its remaining bombs near his Orkney Islands home.

29th — An emergency wartime £1 note is issued (pale blue and orange in colour). The note incorporates a metal security thread for the first time to prevent forgeries. *Fun fact: The note ceased to become legal tender on the 28th May 1962.*

APR

5th — Neville Chamberlain gives a speech to the Conservative Party in London stating he was confident of victory and that Hitler had "missed the bus" by not taking advantage of Germany's military superiority over Britain at the beginning of the war.

5th — Bogskar wins the Grand National horse race by 4 lengths at Aintree Racecourse.

9th — The British campaign in Norway commences following Operation Weserübung, the German invasion of neutral Denmark and Norway.

11th — First Lord of the Admiralty Winston Churchill makes a speech to the House of Commons announcing that the strategically important Faroe Islands, belonging to Denmark, were now being occupied by Britain.

23rd — The War Budget sees taxes and duties increased on income, alcohol, tobacco, telephone calls, telegrams of 'ordinary priority' and postage.

MAY

7-8th	The Norway Debate in the House of Commons sees strong opposition to the Chamberlain war ministry. Chamberlain survives a motion of no confidence by a vote of 281 to 200, but the number of abstentions from within his own Conservative Party causes the level of support for his government to appear very weak, thus making it impossible to continue as Prime Minister.
10th	Neville Chamberlain goes to Buckingham Palace at around 6pm and resigns as Prime Minister of the United Kingdom. King George VI asks Winston Churchill to form the next government and Churchill accepts.
10th	The British invade Iceland with a force of 746 Royal Marines commanded by Colonel Robert Sturges. Meeting no resistance, the troops move quickly to disable communication networks, secure strategic locations, and arrest German citizens. The invasion was carried out to avert a possible German occupation of the island and was in violation of Iceland's neutrality.
13th	Winston Churchill makes his first speech to the House of Commons as Prime Minister stating, "I have nothing to offer but blood, toil, tears, and sweat."
13-14th	Queen Wilhelmina of the Netherlands and her government are evacuated to London using HMS Hereward following the German invasion of the Low Countries.

14th May: The Secretary of State for War, Anthony Eden, gives a radio broadcast announcing the formation of the Local Defence Volunteers (renamed as the Home Guard from the 22nd July) calling for volunteers to join the force; "You will not be paid, but you will receive uniform and will be armed". Eden called on men between the ages of 17 and 65 in Britain, who were not in military service but wished to defend their country against an invasion, to enroll in the LDV at their local police station. It was anticipated that up to 500,000 men might volunteer, and this total number conformed generally with the Army's expectation of the total numbers required to fulfil the functions expected for the new force. But the announcement was met with a great deal of enthusiasm on the part of the population, with 250,000 volunteers attempting to sign up in the first seven days; and by July this number had increased to 1.5 million. *Photo: LDV recruits learning rifle drill at Buckhurst Hill, Essex, July 1940.*

22nd	Parliament passes the Emergency Powers (Defence) Act 1940 putting banks, munitions production, wages, profits and work conditions under the control of the state.
23rd	Parliament passes the Treachery Act 1940 to facilitate the prosecution and execution of enemy spies.
24th	The Anglo-French Supreme War Council decides to withdraw all forces under its control from Norway.

26th May - 4th June: The Dunkirk evacuation of the British Expeditionary Force, code-named Operation Dynamo (also known as the Miracle of Dunkirk), takes place from the beaches and harbour of Dunkirk, in the north of France. The operation commenced after large numbers of Belgian, British and French troops were cut off and surrounded by German troops during the six-week long Battle of France. In a speech to the House of Commons, Prime Minister Winston Churchill called this "a colossal military disaster", saying "the whole root and core and brain of the British Army" had been stranded at Dunkirk and seemed about to perish or be captured. Later in his "we shall fight on the beaches" speech on the 4th of June, he hailed their rescue as a "miracle of deliverance". *Dunkirk evacuation facts: On the first day only 7,669 Allied soldiers were evacuated, but by the end of the eighth day, 338,226 of them had been rescued by a hastily assembled fleet of 861 British and Allied ships (243 of which were sunk during the evacuation). Many troops were able to embark from the harbour's protective mole onto 39 Royal Navy destroyers, four Royal Canadian Navy destroyers, and a variety of civilian merchant ships, while others had to wade out from the beaches, waiting for hours in shoulder-deep water. The BEF lost 68,000 soldiers during the French campaign and had to abandon nearly all of its tanks, vehicles, and equipment. Churchill reminded the country that "we must be very careful not to assign to this deliverance the attributes of a victory. Wars are not won by evacuations."*

JUN

5th	Novelist J. B. Priestley broadcasts his first radio Postscript, "An excursion to hell", marking the role of the pleasure steamers in the Dunkirk Evacuation.
7th	King Haakon VII of Norway and his government are evacuated to London on HMS Devonshire.
10th	Italy declares war on France and the United Kingdom.
11th	The Western Desert Campaign opens with British forces crossing the Frontier Wire into Italian Libya.
12th	After a last stand over 10,000 soldiers of the 51st (Highland) Division, under Major-General Victor Fortune, surrender to Rommel at Saint-Valery-en-Caux.
16th	The Churchill war ministry offers a Franco-British Union to Paul Reynaud, Prime Minister of France, in the hope of preventing France from agreeing to an armistice with Nazi Germany.
17th	RMS Lancastria, serving as a troopship, is bombed and sunk by the Luftwaffe while evacuating British troops and nationals from Saint-Nazaire with the loss of at least 4,000 lives. This is the largest single-ship loss of life in British maritime history; the immense loss of life was such that the British government suppressed news of the disaster - the story was eventually broken on the 25th July in the United States by The New York Times, and in Britain by The Scotsman on the 26th July, more than five weeks after the sinking.
18th	Churchill makes his "This was their finest hour" speech to the House of Commons. It was the third of three speeches which he gave during the period of the Battle of France, and one of the great rallying cries in world history.
23rd	BBC Forces Programme begins broadcasting Music While You Work, a twice daily programme of continuous live popular music broadcast on workdays.
30th	German forces land in Guernsey marking the start of the 5-year Occupation of the Channel Islands.

JUL

2nd	The passenger ship Arandora Star, carrying civilian internees and POWs of Italian and German origin from Liverpool to Canada, is torpedoed and sunk by German submarine U-47 off northwest Ireland with the loss of 865 lives.
3rd	In an attack on Mers-el-Kébir British naval units sink or seize ships of the French fleet anchored in the Algerian ports of Mers El Kébir and Oran. The attack was an attempt to ensure that the Vichy French government would not turn the fleet over to the Germans.
3rd	Cardiff is bombed for the first time. *Cardiff Blitz facts: Between 1940 and the final raid on the city in March 1944, approximately 2,100 bombs fell on Cardiff killing 355 people.*
9th	The Battle of Britain begins. In its opening phase the Luftwaffe attack coastal targets and shipping convoys in the English Channel with the goal of reducing Britain's air defences and naval supply lines ahead of a general air offensive.
19th	Adolf Hitler makes a peace appeal to Britain in an address to the Reichstag. Foreign minister Lord Halifax flatly rejects peace terms in a broadcast reply on the 22nd July.
22nd	The Special Operations Executive is formed under Minister of Economic Warfare Hugh Dalton, to undertake espionage and sabotage in enemy-occupied countries.

9th	Birmingham Blitz (Regenschirm): Heavy bombing of Birmingham begins. *Birmingham Blitz facts: Around 1,852 tons of bombs were dropped on Birmingham during 77 air raids up to the 23rd April 1943. It was the third most heavily bombed city in the United Kingdom in the Second World War, behind London and Liverpool, and resulted in the deaths of 2,241 people.*
18th	"The Hardest Day" in the Battle of Britain: Both sides lose more aircraft combined on this day than at any other point during the campaign as Luftwaffe make an all-out effort to destroy Fighter Command.
18th	HRH Prince Edward, Duke of Windsor, is installed as Governor of the Bahamas.
20th	Churchill pays tribute in Parliament to the Royal Air Force fighter crews: "Never in the field of human conflict was so much owed by so many to so few."
20th	Howard Florey and a team including Ernst Chain at the Sir William Dunn School of Pathology, University of Oxford, publish their laboratory results showing the in vivo bactericidal action of penicillin. *Fun fact: In 1945 Florey and Chain, along with the discoverer of penicillin Alexander Fleming, shared the Nobel Prize in Physiology or Medicine for their development of penicillin.*
25th	The RAF bomb Berlin for the first time. Ninety-five aircraft were dispatched to bomb Tempelhof Airport near the center of Berlin and Siemensstadt, of which 81 dropped their bombs in and around Berlin. While the damage was slight the psychological effect on Hitler was greater. This prompted Hitler to order the shift of the Luftwaffe's target from British airfields and air defences to British cities.

28th August: The first major air raid on Liverpool takes place when 160 bombers attack the city. *Liverpool Blitz facts: By the end of the German raids on Liverpool on the 10th January 1942, their bombs had killed 2,716 people in Liverpool, 442 people in Birkenhead, 409 people in Bootle and 332 people in Wallasey; Over 6,500 homes in Liverpool were completely demolished by aerial bombing and a further 190,000 damaged.*

31st	Actor and director Laurence Olivier and Vivien Leigh are married in California.

7th September: The Blitz begins as 350 bombers drop 300 tonnes of bombs on the docks and streets of the East End of London. London is then systematically bombed by the Luftwaffe for 56 out of the following 57 days and nights. *London Blitz facts: London was targeted a total of 71 times by the Luftwaffe's bombing campaign during the Blitz. During these raids 32,000 civilians in London were killed and 87,000 were seriously injured.*

| 15th | RAF command claims victory over the Luftwaffe in the Battle of Britain; this day has since been known as "Battle of Britain Day". |

SEP

18th	The SS City of Benares is torpedoed by German submarine U-48 in the Atlantic with the loss of 248 of the 406 on board, including 77 of the 90 child evacuees bound for Canada. The sinking caused such public outrage in Britain that it led to Winston Churchill cancelling the Children's Overseas Reception Board (CORB) plan to relocate British children abroad.
24th	King George VI announces the creation of the George Cross decoration during a radio broadcast. *George Cross facts: The George Cross (GC) is the second highest award of the United Kingdom honours system. Since its inception in 1940, the GC has been awarded 408 times, 394 to men, 12 to women, one award to the Island of Malta and another to the Royal Ulster Constabulary (RUC).*
27th	The Battle of Graveney Marsh, Kent: Fighting takes place between the crew of a shot-down German Junkers Ju 88 bomber and a detachment of soldiers from the 1st Battalion London Irish Rifles in Seasalter. The aircraft crew initially resist arrest with gunfire but surrender after one of the airmen is shot in the foot. *Interesting fact: This was the last ground engagement involving a foreign force to take place on the mainland of Great Britain.*

OCT

9th	Winston Churchill succeeds Neville Chamberlain as Leader of the Conservative Party.
14th	At least 64 people are killed when a German bomb penetrates Balham station on the London Underground which is in use as an air-raid shelter.
25th	Air Chief Marshal Sir Charles Portal is appointed to succeed Sir Cyril Newall as Chief of the Air Staff, a post he will hold for the remainder of the War.
31st	The Battle of Britain ends.

NOV

9th	A major fire destroys a large part of Castle Howard in Yorkshire. The fire takes the Malton and York Fire Brigades eight hours to bring under control.
11th	Battle of Taranto: The Royal Navy, under Admiral Andrew Cunningham, launches the first aircraft carrier strike in history on the Italian fleet at Taranto. The success of this attack augured the ascendancy of naval aviation over the big guns of battleships.
14th	The centre of Coventry is destroyed by 515 German Luftwaffe bombers: 150,000 incendiary devices, 503 tons of high explosives and 130 parachute mines level 60,000 of the city's 75,000 buildings. At least 568 people are killed, while 863 more are injured - it is the most severe raid on Coventry during the war. Exceptionally, the location and nature of the damage here is immediately publicised in the media.
17th	Operation White, an attempt to deliver fourteen aircraft from the carrier HMS Argus to Malta, takes place. Only five planes make it due to bad weather and the presence of the Italian Fleet.
19th	Less than a week after the blitz of Coventry, further heavy air raids take place in central England. Birmingham, West Bromwich, Dudley and Tipton are all bombed. Some 900 people are killed and 2,000 more injured.

NOV

23rd	Heavy bombing by the Luftwaffe occurs over Southampton; 77 people are killed and more than 300 injured.
24th	148 Luftflotte 3 bombers leave Germany to bomb Bristol and drop around 12,000 incendiary bombs and 160 tons of high-explosive bombs.
25th	The de Havilland Mosquito makes its first flight. The twin-engined combat aircraft was unusual in that its frame was constructed almost entirely of wood. *Fun fact: It was nicknamed The Wooden Wonder, or "Mossie" to its crews.*

DEC

12-15th	Sheffield Blitz (Operation Crucible): The city of Sheffield is heavily bombed by the Luftwaffe. 660 people are killed while another 1,500 are injured and some 30,000 more left homeless.
17th	The Royal Navy's A-class destroyer HMS Acheron hits a mine off the Isle of Wight and sinks within four minutes. 196 crewmen and yard workers, who were on board for a post refit trial, were killed; there were just 19 survivors. *Further information: The wreck site of HMS Acheron was designated as a Protected Place under the Protection of Military Remains Act 1986 in 2006.*
20th	An anti-aircraft shell fired from Dudley accidentally strikes the Boat Inn public house in neighbouring Tipton, fatally injuring 12 people at a wedding reception (including the bride, while the groom lost both legs) as well as the resident of an adjacent house.
20th	Two Spitfire fighters of No.66 Squadron attack Le Touquet in France, strafing targets of opportunity such as power transformers. This tactic, codenamed Rhubarb, marked a shift in RAF tactics to a more offensive role.
22nd	Manchester is heavily bombed as the Luftwaffe air raids on Britain continue. 363 people are killed and 1,183 wounded; Manchester Cathedral is badly damaged.
24th	An unofficial two-day Christmas truce begins in the aerial war between Britain and Germany.
29th	Approximately 100,000 bombs fall on the city of London, dropped by 136 German bombers. The heavy bombing was one of the most destructive air raids of the Blitz and resulted in, what has become known as, the Second Great Fire of London.

POPULAR BRITISH PUBLICATIONS 1940

- Michael Foot, Frank Owen and Peter Howard's political tract Guilty Men (published under the pseudonym "Cato").
- Joyce Carey's novel Charley is My Darling.
- Agatha Christie's Hercule Poirot novels Sad Cypress and One, Two, Buckle My Shoe.
- T. S. Eliot's poem East Coker, second of the Four Quartets.
- Graham Greene's novel The Power and the Glory.
- Michael Sadleir's novel Fanny by Gaslight
- C. P. Snow's novel George Passant.
- C. Henry Warren's account England is a Village.

1. 2nd January: The Irish government introduces emergency powers to extend the power of internment from foreign nationals to Irish citizens, and to allow juryless court martials of civilians. These were in response to increased activity by the Irish Republican Army (IRA).

2. 9th February: Joe Louis defeats Arturo Godoy by split decision at Madison Square Garden in New York City to retain his Ring and world heavyweight boxing titles. He would defend these titles a further 3 times in 1940 against Johnny Paychek, Arturo Godoy (rematch), and Al McCoy. *Interesting facts: In all, Louis made 25 defences of his heavyweight title from 1937 to 1948, and was a world champion for 11 years and 10 months. His most remarkable record is that he knocked out 23 opponents in 27 title fights, including five world champions. Photo 1: Godoy and Louis on CBS Radio's We, the People human interest program. Photo 2: Louis and Godoy in their rematch on June 20 - Louis won by a technical knockout in the eighth round.*

3. 20th February: Tom and Jerry make their debut in the short film Puss Gets the Boot (under their original names of Jasper and Jinx). The cartoon was directed by William Hanna, Joseph Barbera and Rudolf Ising, and produced by Rudolf Ising and Fred Quimby.

4. 27th February: Martin Kamen and Sam Ruben discover the radioactive isotope carbon-14 at the University of California Radiation Laboratory, Berkeley, U.S. *Interesting fact: Its presence in organic materials is the basis of the radiocarbon dating method pioneered by Willard Libby and colleagues (1949) to date archaeological, geological and hydrogeological samples.*

5. 29th February: The 12th Academy Awards, celebrating the best in film from 1939, are held in Los Angeles and are hosted by Bob Hope (his first of nineteen ceremonies). Gone With The Wind won eight awards including Best Picture. Robert Donat and Vivien Leigh won the best actor and actress awards, and Hattie McDaniel became the first African-American to win an Oscar when she was named Best Supporting Actress. *Fun facts: The Los Angeles Times published the names of the winners in its 8:45pm edition so most of the attendees already knew the results ahead of time. The Academy responded by starting a tradition the following year in which the winners were not revealed until the ceremony itself when sealed envelopes were opened.*

6. 20th March: The entire French cabinet resign. Although Prime Minister Édouard Daladier had won a vote of confidence in the Chamber of Deputies 239-1, there were so many abstentions among the 551 members that he recognised the vote as a defeat.

7. 26th March: A federal election was held in Canada and the Liberal government of William Lyon Mackenzie King was re-elected to another majority government.

8. 9th April: At 5:20am in Norway (4:20am in Denmark), the German envoys in Oslo and Copenhagen presented the Norwegian and Danish governments with a German ultimatum demanding that they immediately accept the "protection of the Reich." Denmark capitulated so as to not provoke mass bloodshed at the hands of the Germans, and the country was invaded in six hours. Norwegian Foreign Affairs Minister Halvdan Koht, however, responded with the defiant words "Vi gir oss ikke frivillig, kampen er allerede i gang" ("We will not submit voluntarily; the struggle is already underway"). The entire Norwegian government, including King Haakon VII, fled the capital that morning for the mountains in the north.

9. 24th April: Issue No.1 of the DC comic book Batman is published. This first issue marked the debut of the Joker and Catwoman (initially called The Cat). *Fun fact: A near mint copy (graded 9.2 grade by CGC) sold at auction for $567,625 in August 2013.*

10. 29th April: Helsinki forfeits the 1940 Summer Olympics and just a week later (on the 6th May) the International Olympic Committee formally cancels them. The Olympics would not resume again until the London Games in 1948.

11. 10th May: A massive German offensive sees them invade Belgium, France, Luxembourg and the Netherlands; the United States freezes Belgian, Dutch and Luxembourger assets to keep them out of Germany's hands.

12. 25th May: The Crypt of Civilization at Oglethorpe University in Brookhaven, Georgia, U.S. is sealed. *Fun facts: The 2,000-cubic-foot (57-cubic-meter) room contains numerous artefacts and documents, and is designed for opening in the year 8113 AD. During the 50th anniversary year of its sealing, the Guinness Book of World Records cited the crypt as the "first successful attempt to bury a record of this culture for any future inhabitants or visitors to the planet Earth." Photo: An image of The Crypt and its creator, Oglethorpe University president Dr. Thornwell Jacobs.*

13. | 18th June: General Charles de Gaulle, de facto leader of the Free French Forces, makes his first broadcast appeal over Radio Londres rallying French Resistance.

14. 27th July: Bugs Bunny makes his official debut in the Oscar-nominated cartoon short, A Wild Hare. *Fun facts: The prototypical version of Bugs Bunny appeared in four cartoons before making his official debut in 1940. Bugs Bunny has also appeared in more films than any other cartoon character and has his own star on the Hollywood Walk of Fame. Pictured: Bugs Bunny's evolution from 'Happy Rabbit' in 1938 to the present day.*

15. | 23rd August: The musical drama film Young People, starring 12-year-old Shirley Temple, premieres at the Roxy Theatre in New York City. This was Temple's final film for 20th Century Fox and it was thought at that time that it might be her last film ever. She actually went on to make 13 more films, the last being A Kiss for Corliss (1949).

16. | 2nd September: An agreement between America and Great Britain is announced to the effect that 50 U.S. destroyers, needed for escort work, will be transferred to Great Britain. In return America gains 99-year leases on British bases in the North Atlantic, West Indies and Bermuda.

17. | 12th September: Prehistoric paintings are discovered in a cave in Lascaux near Montignac, France, by 18-year-old Marcel Ravidat.

18. | 26th September: The United States imposes a total embargo on all scrap metal shipments to Japan. The reasons were due to Japan's move into Indochina combined with its war with China, withdrawal from the League of Nations, alliance with Germany and Italy, and increasing militarisation. The embargo hits Japan's economy particularly hard.

19. | 2nd November: In one of the most extraordinary aviation incidents of the war Greek Air Force pilot Marinos Mitralexis, after running out of ammunition, brings down and Italian bomber by ramming its rudder and sending it out of control. He then makes an emergency landing near the crashed bomber. Having landed, Mitralexis proceeds to arrest the four surviving crew members of the enemy aircraft, who had parachuted to safety, using his pistol. *Bravery: For this extraordinary feat, Mitralexis was promoted and awarded a number of medals, including Greece's highest award for bravery, the Gold Cross of Valour.*

20. | 5th November: Franklin D. Roosevelt defeats Republican challenger Wendell Willkie to become the United States president for an unprecedented third time.

21. | 10th November: The Copacabana nightclub opens in New York City. *Fun facts: Many entertainers such as Danny Thomas, Pat Cooper, and the comedy team of Dean Martin and Jerry Lewis made their New York debuts at the Copacabana.*

BIRTHS
U.K. PERSONALITIES
BORN IN 1940

Michael Reid

b. 19th January 1940
d. 29th July 2007

Comedian, actor, author and occasional television presenter from London who is noted for his gravelly voice and strong Cockney accent. His first work in entertainment was as a stand-up comedian in clubs and aboard cruise liners in the early 1960s. In the 1970's he became one of the original stars of the popular TV series The Comedians. Reid is probably best remembered though for his role as Frank Butcher in the BBC soap opera EastEnders (1987-2005).

Sir John Vincent Hurt, CBE

b. 22nd January 1940
d. 25th January 2017

Actor whose screen and stage career spanned more than 50 years. Regarded as one of Britain's finest actors Hurt came to prominence for his role as Richard Rich in the film A Man For All Seasons (1966) and gained BAFTA Award nominations for his roles in 10 Rillington Place (1971) and The Naked Civil Servant (1975); winning his first BAFTA for the latter. In 2012 he was honoured with the Lifetime Achievement BAFTA Award and was knighted in 2015 for his services to drama.

Sir David John White, OBE

b. 2nd February 1940

Actor known professionally by his stage name David Jason. He is best known for his roles as Derek 'Del Boy' Trotter in Only Fools And Horses, and Detective Inspector Jack Frost in the ITV crime drama A Touch Of Frost. Other high-profile television roles have been Granville in the sitcom Open All Hours, and Pop Larkin in the comedy drama The Darling Buds of May. Jason has won four BAFTAs, four British Comedy Awards, and seven National Television Awards during his career to date.

James Joseph Tarbuck, OBE

b. 6th February 1940

Comedian, singer and television personality who is known for hosting Sunday Night at the London Palladium in the mid-1960s, and for his numerous game and quiz shows during the 1970s, '80s and early '90s. In the 1980s he also notably hosted a number of Sunday night variety shows such as Live From Her Majesty's, Live from the Piccadilly, and Live from the Palladium. Tarbuck was awarded the OBE in the 1994 Queen's New Year Honours List for his services to charity.

Mary Denise Rand, MBE

b. 10th February 1940

Former track and field athlete who won the long jump at the 1964 Tokyo Summer Olympics by breaking the world record, and at the same time became the first British female to win an Olympic gold medal in track and field. At Tokyo she also won a bronze in the 4x 100 relay and a silver in the Pentathlon (her 5035 points putting her second in the all-time rankings). Rand was made an MBE in the 1965 New Year's Honours List and was inducted into the England Athletics Hall of Fame in 2009.

James Peter Greaves

b. 20th February 1940

Former England international footballer who began his professional career at Chelsea in 1957. He is England's fourth highest international goal scorer (44 goals), Tottenham Hotspur's highest ever goal scorer (266 goals), the highest goal scorer in the history of English top-flight football (357 goals), and has also scored more hat-tricks (six) for England than anyone else. Greaves finished as the First Division's top scorer in six seasons and is a member of the English Football Hall of Fame.

Denis Law, CBE

b. 24th February 1940

Former Scottish footballer whose career began at Second Division Huddersfield Town in 1956. He played for Manchester City and Torino in Italy before signing for Manchester United in 1962 (for a British record transfer fee of £115,000). Law spent 11 years at United scoring 237 goals in 404 appearances. His goals tally places him third in the club's history, behind Wayne Rooney and Bobby Charlton. Law also played for Scotland a total of 55 times and scored a joint record 30 goals.

Frank Gordon Dobson

b. 15th March 1940

British Labour Party politician who was the Member of Parliament (MP) for Holborn and St. Pancras from 1979 to 2015. His naturally pugnacious style of politics earned him rapid promotion to the front bench where he worked in several important posts from 1982. Under Prime Minister Tony Blair he served in the Cabinet as Secretary of State for Health (1997-1999) and in 2000 was the official Labour Party candidate for Mayor of London.

Stanley Michael Bailey Hailwood, MBE, GM

b. 2nd April 1940
d. 23rd March 1981

Motorcycle road racer who is regarded by many as one of the greatest racers of all time. He was known as 'Mike the Bike' because of his natural riding ability on bikes with a range of engine capacities. By the time he had retired he had achieved an impressive 76 Grand Prix victories, 112 Grand Prix podiums, 14 Isle of Man TT wins and 9 World Championships. Hailwood also competed in Formula One and other classes of car racing during his career.

Dame Penelope Anne Constance Keith, DBE, DL

b. 2nd April 1940

Actress active in all genres including radio, stage, television and film. She is primarily known for her roles in the sitcoms The Good Life, and To the Manor Born. After these she went on to star in a number of other sitcoms including Executive Stress, No Job for a Lady, and Next of Kin. She succeeded Lord Olivier as president of the Actors' Benevolent Fund after his death in 1989, and was appointed a Dame in the 2014 New Year Honours for services to the arts and to charity.

Jeffrey Howard Archer, Baron Archer of Weston-super-Mare

b. 15th April 1940

Novelist and former politician. Before becoming an author he was an MP for Louth, Lincolnshire (1969-1974) but did not seek re-election after a financial scandal that left him almost bankrupt. He revived his fortunes as a best-selling novelist; his books have sold around 330 million copies worldwide. Archer became deputy chairman of the Conservative Party in the mid-1980s and was made a life peer in 1992. His political career ended in 2001 when he was imprisoned for perjury and perverting the course of justice.

Ronald Wycherley

b. 17th April 1940
d. 28th January 1983

Singer and songwriter from the late 1950s to the mid-1960s who was better known by his stage name Billy Fury. An early British rock and roll (and film) star, he equalled the Beatles' record of 24 hits in the 1960s, and spent 332 weeks on the UK chart, without a chart-topping single or album. In 2003 a bronze statue of Fury was unveiled at the National Museum of Liverpool Life - the sculpture was donated by 'The Sound of Fury' fan club with money raised by fans.

Angela Olive Carter-Pearce (née Stalker)

b. 7th May 1940
d. 16th February 1992

Novelist, short story writer and journalist known for her feminist, magical realism, and picaresque works. She is best remembered for her book The Bloody Chamber which was published in 1979. In 2008, The Times ranked Carter tenth in their list of 'The 50 greatest British writers since 1945'. In 2012, Nights at the Circus (published in 1984) was selected as the best ever winner of the James Tait Black Memorial Prize.

Sir Thomas John Woodward, OBE

b. 7th June 1940

Welsh singer, known professionally as Tom Jones, whose career has spanned six decades from his emergence as a vocalist in the mid-1960s. He has sold over 100 million records, with thirty-six Top 40 hits in the UK and nineteen in the US. His awards include a Grammy for Best New Artist (1966) and two Brits: Best British Male (2000) and Outstanding Contribution to Music (2003). Jones was made an OBE in 1999 and in 2006 he was knighted by the Queen for services to music.

Terence Nelhams-Wright

b. 23rd June 1940
d. 8th March 2003

British teen idol, singer, actor and financial journalist better known as Adam Faith. He was one of the most charted acts of the 1960s and became the first UK artist to lodge his initial seven hits in the Top 5. He was also one of the first British acts to regularly record original songs. At the end of the 1960s he left the record industry to concentrate fully on fulfilling his acting ambitions. Over the next 34 years Faith was to become one of the UKs most popular stars of stage and screen.

Sir Richard Starkey, MBE

b. 7th July 1940

Musician, singer, songwriter and actor known professionally as Ringo Starr. He gained worldwide fame as the drummer for the Beatles, today regarded as the foremost and most influential music band in history. He was inducted into the Rock and Roll Hall of Fame as a Beatle in 1988, and again in 2015 for his solo career (making him one of just 21 performers inducted more than once). Starr was appointed a Knight Bachelor in the 2018 New Year Honours for services to music.

Sir Patrick Stewart, OBE

b. 13th July 1940

Actor whose career has spanned almost six decades and has included roles on stage, television and film. He has twice received the Laurence Olivier Award for Best Actor in a Supporting Role; for his performances in Antony and Cleopatra (1979) and Hamlet (2008). In film and television Stewart has had prominent leading roles such as Captain Jean-Luc Picard in Star Trek: The Next Generation and its successor films, and as Professor Charles Xavier in the X-Men series of superhero films.

Timothy Julian Brooke-Taylor, OBE

b. 17th July 1940

Actor who first became known to the public for his work on BBC Radio with I'm Sorry, I'll Read That Again, before moving into television with At Last the 1948 Show (working together with old Cambridge friends John Cleese and Graham Chapman). He is probably best known though as a member of The Goodies, starring in the television series throughout the 1970s. He has been a panellist on BBC radios' comedy panel game 'I'm Sorry I Haven't a Clue' for over 40 years.

Dame Zandra Lindsey Rhodes, DBE, RDI

b. 19th September 1940

Fashion designer who was one of the new wave of British designers who put London at the forefront of the international fashion scene in the 1970s. Rhodes designed for Diana, Princess of Wales, and continues to design for royalty and celebrities - she notably designed several famous costumes for Freddie Mercury and Brian May of Queen. Rhodes was appointed a CBE in 1997, and in 2014 became Dame in the Queen's Birthday Honours for services to British fashion and textiles.

John Winston Ono Lennon, MBE

b. 9th October 1940
d. 8th December 1980

Singer, songwriter, and peace activist who co-founded the Beatles, the most commercially successful band in the history of popular music. After the Beatles disbanded in 1970 he pursued a solo career and started the band Plastic Ono Band with his second wife Yoko Ono. Since his death in 1982 Lennon has been inducted into both the Songwriters Hall of Fame (1987) and the Rock and Roll Hall of Fame (twice); in 1988 as a member of the Beatles and in 1994 as a solo artist.

Sir Cliff Richard, OBE

b. 14th October 1940

British pop singer, musician, performer, actor and philanthropist born Harry Rodger Webb. With his backing group, the Shadows, Richard dominated the British popular music scene in the late 1950s to early 1960s. He has had 67 UK top ten singles, has achieved 14 UK No.1 singles and has sold more than 250 million records worldwide. Richard is also the only singer to have had a No.1 record in the UK in five consecutive decades. In 1995 he was invested a Knight Bachelor by the Queen.

Peter James Stringfellow

b. 17th October 1940
d. 7th June 2018

English businessman who owned several nightclubs. His business career running clubs began after he was unable to find work due to a conviction and imprisonment for selling stolen carpets. In 1980 he opened Stringfellows in Covent Garden. It was an immediate success as a nightclub with celebrities, international film stars, TV personalities, rock stars and models. In addition to his club in London he also opened others in New York, Miami and Los Angeles.

Sir Michael John Gambon, CBE

b. 19th October 1940

Irish-born British actor who has worked in theatre, television, and film. He has played the eponymous mystery writer protagonist in the BBC television serial The Singing Detective, Jules Maigret in the 1990s ITV serial Maigret, and Professor Albus Dumbledore in the final six Harry Potter films. He has won four BAFTA TV Awards and three Olivier Awards. Gambon was knighted in 1998 for services to drama and was awarded the Irish Film & Television Academy Lifetime Achievement Award in 2017 for his contribution to Irish film.

NOTABLE DEATHS

11th Feb	John Buchan, 1st Baron Tweedsmuir, GCMG, GCVO, CH, PC (b. 26th August 1875) - Scottish novelist, historian and Unionist politician who served as Governor General of Canada.
29th Feb	Edward Frederic Benson (b. 24th July 1867) - Novelist, biographer, memoirist, archaeologist and short story writer.
18th Apr	Herbert Albert Laurens Fisher, OM, PC, FRS, FBA (b. 21st March 1865) - Historian, educator and Liberal politician who served as President of the Board of Education in David Lloyd George's 1916-1922 coalition government.
2nd May	Ernest Edward Mills Joyce, AM (b. 1875) - Royal Naval seaman and explorer who participated in four Antarctic expeditions, serving under both Robert Falcon Scott and Ernest Shackleton.
7th May	George Lansbury (b. 22nd February 1859) - Politician and social reformer who led the Labour Party from 1932 to 1935.
6th Jun	Edward Erskholme Clive (b. 28th August 1879) - Welsh stage actor and director who had a prolific acting career in Britain and America.
17th Jun	Sir Arthur Harden, FRS (b. 12th October 1865) - Biochemist who shared the Nobel Prize in Chemistry in 1929 with Hans von Euler-Chelpin (for their investigations into the fermentation of sugar and fermentative enzymes).
24th Jun	Alfred Fowler, CBE, FRS (b. 22nd March 1868) - Astronomer who was president of the Royal Astronomical Society from 1919 to 1921.
15th Jul	Donald Esme Clayton Calthrop (b. 11th April 1888) - Stage and film actor who appeared in 63 films between 1916 and 1940, including five films directed by Alfred Hitchcock.
16th Jul	Ray Strachey (b. Rachel Pearsall Conn Costelloe; 4th June 1887) - Feminist politician, artist and writer.
22nd Aug	Sir Oliver Joseph Lodge, FRS (b. 12th June 1851) - Physicist and writer involved in the development of, and holder of key patents for, radio. Lodge was Principal of the University of Birmingham from 1900 to 1920.
30th Aug	Sir Joseph John Thomson, OM, PRS (b. 18th December 1856) - Physicist and Nobel Laureate credited with the discovery and identification of the electron.
26th Sep	William Henry Davies (b. 3rd July 1871) - Welsh poet and writer who spent a significant part of his life as a tramp in the United Kingdom and United States.
9th Oct	Sir Wilfred Thomason Grenfell, KCMG (b. 28th February 1865) - Physician, medical missionary, social reformer and author.
30th Oct	Hilda Matheson, OBE (b. 7th June 1888) - Pioneering radio talks producer who served as the first Director of Talks at the BBC between 1927 and 1931.
1st Nov	Squadron Leader Archibald Ashmore McKellar, DSO, DFC & Bar (b. 10th April 1912) - Royal Air Force flying ace during the Second World War.
9th Nov	Arthur Neville Chamberlain, FRS (b. 18th March 1869) - Conservative Party statesman who served as Prime Minister from May 1937 to May 1940.
24th Nov	James Craig, 1st Viscount Craigavon, PC, PC (NI), DL (b. 8th January 1871) - Prominent Irish unionist politician, leader of the Ulster Unionist Party and the first Prime Minister of Northern Ireland. He was created a baronet in 1918 and raised to the Peerage in 1927.
16th Dec	William Wallace (b. 3rd July 1860) - Scottish classical composer and writer who served as Dean of the Faculty of Music in the University of London.

POPULAR MUSIC

Glenn Miller	No.1	In The Mood
Cliff Edwards (Ukelele Ike)	No.2	When You Wish Upon A Star
The Ink Spots	No.3	Whispering Grass
Bing Crosby	No.4	Only Forever
Artie Shaw	No.5	All The Things You Are
George Formby	No.6	Bless 'Em All
Vera Lynn	No.7	A Nightingale Sang In Berkeley Square
Bert Ambrose & His Orchestra	No.8	The Singing Hills
Leslie Hutchinson	No.9	The Woodpecker Song
Hal Kemp	No.10	In An 18th Century Drawing Room

N.B. During this era music was dominated by a number of 'Big Bands' and songs could be attributed to the band leader, the band name, the lead singer or a combination of these. On top of this the success of a song was tied to the sales of sheet music, so a popular song would often be perfomed by many different combinations of singers and bands, and the contemporary charts would list the song without clarifying whose version was the major hit. With this in mind it should be noted that although the above chart has been compiled with best intent it remains subjective.

1. Glenn Miller
In The Mood

Label:	Written by:	Length:
HMV	Razaf / Garland	3 mins 29 secs

Alton Glenn Miller (b. 1st March 1904 - MIA 15th December 1944) was a big-band musician, arranger, composer and bandleader in the swing era. He was the best-selling recording artist from 1939 to 1943, leading one of the best-known big bands and scoring 23 No.1 hits. In The Mood became an anthem of the times and sold over 60 million records, the most of any swing band. In 1983 the song was inducted into the Grammy Hall of Fame and 2004 into the U.S. Library of Congress National Recording Registry.

2. Cliff Edwards
When You Wish Upon A Star

Label:	Written by:	Length:
HMV	Harline / Washington	3 mins 17 secs

Clifton Avon Edwards (b. 14th June 1895 - d. 17th July 1971) was a musician, singer, actor and voice actor, otherwise known as 'Ukulele Ike', who enjoyed considerable popularity in the 1920s and early 1930s. When You Wish Upon a Star was written for Walt Disney's 1940 adaptation of Pinocchio and was sung by Edwards in the character of Jiminy Cricket. The song won the 1940 Academy Award for Best Original Song and was inducted into the Grammy Hall of Fame in 2002.

3 The Ink Spots
Whispering Grass

Label:	Written by:	Length:
Brunswick	Fred & Doris Fisher	2 mins 39 secs

The Ink Spots, Bill Kenny (b. 12th June 1914 - d. 23rd March 1978), Deek Watson (b. 18th July 1909 - d. 4th November 1969), Charlie Fuqua (b. 20th October 1910 - d. 21st December 1971), and Hoppy Jones (b. 17th February 1905 - d. 18th October 1944), were a pop vocal group who gained international fame in the 1930s and 1940s. In 1989 the Ink Spots were inducted into the Rock and Roll Hall of Fame, and in 1999 they were inducted into the Vocal Group Hall of Fame.

4 Bing Crosby
Only Forever

Label:	Written by:	Length:
Decca	Monaco / Burke	3 mins 12 secs

Harry Lillis 'Bing' Crosby, Jr. (b. 3rd May 1903 - d. 14th October 1977) was a singer and actor. Crosby's trademark warm bass-baritone voice made him the best-selling recording artist of the 20th century selling close to a billion records, tapes, compact discs and digital downloads worldwide. Only Forever was written by James V. Monaco and Johnny Burke for the 1940 film Rhythm On The River, and was nominated for the Academy Award for Best Original Song.

Artie Shaw
All The Things You Are

Label:	Written by:	Length:
Victor	Hammerstein II / Kern	3 mins 12 secs

Artie Shaw (b. Arthur Jacob Arshawsky; 23rd May 1910 - d. 30th December 2004) was a clarinettist, composer, bandleader, author and actor. Widely regarded as one of jazz's finest clarinettists, Shaw led one of the most popular big bands of the late 1930s through the early 1940s. All The Things You Are was originally composed for the musical Very Warm For May (1939); Helen Forrest (b. Helen Fogel; 12th April 1917 - d. 11th July 1999) was the vocalist.

George Formby
Bless 'Em All

Label:	Written by:	Length:
Regal Zonophone	Hughes / Lake / Stillman	3 mins 2 secs

George Hoy Booth Formby, OBE (b. 26th May 1904 - d. 6th March 1961) was an actor, singer-songwriter and comedian who became known to a worldwide audience through his films of the 1930s and 1940s. On stage, screen and record, he sang light comical songs, usually playing the ukulele or banjolele, and became the UK's highest-paid entertainer.

7 Vera Lynn
A Nightingale Sang In Berkeley Square

Label:	**Written by:**	**Length:**
HMV / Decca	Maschwitz / Connor	3 mins 55 secs

Dame Vera Margaret Lynn, CH DBE OStJ (née Welch; b. 20th March 1917), widely known as 'the Forces' Sweetheart', is a singer, songwriter and actress, whose musical recordings and performances were enormously popular during World War 2. During the war she toured Egypt, India and Burma as part of ENSA, giving outdoor concerts for the troops. A Nightingale Sang in Berkeley Square was written shortly before the outbreak of the Second World War and was recorded by many artists at the time including Judy Campbell, Ray Nobel, Glenn Miller and Guy Lombardo.

8 Bert Ambrose & His Orchestra
The Singing Hills

Label:	**Written by:**	**Length:**
Decca	Sanford / David / Mysels	2 mins 45 secs

Benjamin Baruch Ambrose (b. 11th September 1896 - d. 11th June 1971) was known professionally as Ambrose or Bert Ambrose. He was an English bandleader and violinist who became the leader of the highly acclaimed British dance band Bert Ambrose & His Orchestra in the 1930s.

9 Leslie Hutchinson
The Woodpecker Song

Label:	Written by:	Length:
Parlophone	Adamson / Lazzaro	2 mins 54 secs

Leslie Arthur Julien 'Hutch' Hutchinson (b. 7th March 1900 - d. 18th August 1969) was a Grenada-born singer and pianist who was one of the biggest cabaret stars in the world during the 1920s and 1930s. Hutchinson came to England in 1927 and was regularly heard on air with the BBC. He was one of the first stars in Britain to volunteer to entertain the troops at home and abroad during World War II.

10 Hal Kemp
In An 18th Century Drawing Room

Label:	Written by:	Length:
HMV	Raymond Scott	2 mins 44 secs

James Hal Kemp (b. 27th March 1904 - d. 21st December 1940) was a jazz alto saxophonist, clarinettist, bandleader, composer, and arranger. Kemp was inducted into the Big Band and Jazz Hall of Fame in 1992.

1940: TOP FILMS

1. **Rebecca** - *United Artists*
2. **The Philadelphia Story** - *MGM*
3. **The Grapes Of Wrath** - *20th Century-Fox*
4. **The Great Dictator** - *United Artists*
5. **Pinocchio** - *Disney*

OSCARS

Best Picture: Rebecca
Most Nominations: Rebecca (11)
Most Wins: The Thief of Bagdad (3)

Photo 1: James Stewart and Ginger Rogers with their Oscars for best actor and actress.
Photo 2: Alfred Lunt and Lynn Fontanne congratulating Jane Darwell (center right) and Walter Brennan (far right) for their Academy Award wins.

Best Director: John Ford - *The Grapes of Wrath*

Best Actor: James Stewart - *The Philadelphia Story*
Best Actress: Ginger Rogers - *Kitty Foyle*
Best Supporting Actor: Walter Brennan - *The Westerner*
Best Supporting Actress: Jane Darwell - *The Grapes of Wrath*

The 13th Academy Awards were presented on the 27th February 1941.

REBECCA

Directed by: Alfred Hitchcock - Runtime: 2 hours 10 minutes

Maxim de Winter, still troubled by the death of his first wife Rebecca, falls in love with a shy ladies' companion. They get married but the second Mrs. de Winter soon discovers that Rebecca still has a strange hold on everyone in the house…

STARRING

Laurence Olivier
Born: 22nd May 1907
Died: 11th July 1989

Character:
Maxim de Winter

Actor and director who, along with his contemporaries Ralph Richardson, Peggy Ashcroft and John Gielgud, dominated the British stage of the mid-20th century. He also worked in films throughout his career and received four Academy Awards, two British Academy Film Awards, five Emmy Awards and three Golden Globe Awards. He is commemorated today in the Laurence Olivier Awards, given annually by the Society of London Theatre.

Joan Fontaine
Born: 22nd October 1917
Died: 15th December 2013

Character:
Mrs. de Winter

American actress born Joan de Beauvoir de Havilland (in Japan, to British parents) who was best known for her starring roles in cinema during the Classical Hollywood era. Fontaine appeared in more than 45 feature films in a career that spanned five decades. She was nominated three times for an Academy Award, winning once for her role in Alfred Hitchcock's Suspicion (1941) - her other nominated roles were in the films Rebecca and The Constant Nymph (1943).

George Sanders
Born: 3rd July 1906
Died: 25th April 1972

Character:
Jack Favell

Film and television actor, singer-songwriter, music composer, and author. His career as an actor spanned over forty years. His upper-class English accent and bass voice often led him to be cast as sophisticated but villainous characters. He is perhaps best known for his roles in Rebecca, Foreign Correspondent (1940), All About Eve (1950), for which he won an Academy Award, and as Simon Templar, 'The Saint', in five films made in the 1930s and 1940s.

TRIVIA

Goofs

At the inquest when Ben begins to testify the clock reads 11:48, but a few minutes later when Mr. de Winter is recalled it reads 1:53. Shortly after, when Mrs de Winter faints, the clock reads 11:48 once again.

The large map on the courtroom wall depicts the Americas and as such it is implausible that it would be displayed on the wall of an English courtroom.

Interesting Facts

Rebecca was the first film that Sir Alfred Hitchcock made in Hollywood and was the only one that won a Best Picture Academy Award. His other Oscar nominated works were Lifeboat (1944), Spellbound (1945), Rear Window (1954) and Psycho (1960).

CONTINUED

Interesting Facts Over twenty actresses were screen-tested for the role of Mrs. de Winter, which eventually went to newcomer Joan Fontaine.

Because Sir Laurence Olivier wanted his then-girlfriend Vivien Leigh to play the lead role, he treated Joan Fontaine horribly. This shook Fontaine up quite a bit, so Sir Alfred Hitchcock decided to capitalise on this by telling her everyone on the set hated her, thus making her shy and uneasy, just what he wanted from her performance.

Filming started five days after the U.K. entered World War II. This proved to be particularly troublesome to Sir Alfred Hitchcock and the movie's largely British cast.

Due to the success of the film in Spain the specific jackets worn by Joan Fontaine during filming began to be known as 'rebecas'. The word is still used nowadays to refer to this item of clothing.

Quote **Maxim de Winter:** I can't forget what it's done to you. I've been thinking of nothing else since it happened. It's gone forever, that funny young, lost look I loved won't ever come back. I killed that when I told you about Rebecca. It's gone. In a few hours, you've grown so much older.

THE PHILADELPHIA STORY

Directed by: George Cukor - Runtime: 1 hour 52 minutes

When a rich woman's ex-husband and a tabloid-type reporter turn up just before her planned remarriage, she begins to learn the truth about herself.

STARRING

Cary Grant
Born: 18th January 1904
Died: 29th November 1986

Character:
C. K. Dexter Haven

British-American actor (born Archibald Alec Leach) known as one of classic Hollywood's definitive leading men. He began a career in Hollywood in the early 1930s and became known for his transatlantic accent, light-hearted approach to acting, comic timing and debonair demeanour. He was twice nominated for the Academy Award for Best Actor for his roles in Penny Serenade (1941) and None But The Lonely Heart (1944).

Katharine Hepburn
Born: 12th May 1907
Died: 29th June 2003

Character:
Tracy Lord

American actress known for her fierce independence and spirited personality. Hepburn was a leading lady in Hollywood for more than 60 years and appeared in a range of genres from screwball comedy to literary drama, and she received a record of four Academy Awards for Best Actress. In 1999, Hepburn was named by the American Film Institute as the greatest female star of Classic Hollywood Cinema.

James Stewart
Born: 20th May 1908
Died: 2nd July 1997

Character:
Macaulay Connor

Actor and military officer who is among the most honoured and popular stars in film history. With a career spanning 62 years, Stewart was nominated for five Academy Awards, winning one for The Philadelphia Story and receiving another, a Lifetime Achievement award, in 1985. In 1999, Stewart was named the third-greatest male screen legend of the Golden Age of Hollywood by the American Film Institute, behind Humphrey Bogart and Cary Grant.

TRIVIA

Goofs	When CK Dexter-Haven is whistling after coming to the mansion, Mrs. Lord calls Tracy 'Kathy' instead of Tracy.
	As Connor and Tracy exit the library the boom mic is reflected on the windscreen of Tracy's car.
Interesting Facts	James Stewart never felt he deserved the Oscar for his performance in this film, especially since he had initially felt miscast. He always maintained that Henry Fonda should have won instead for The Grapes Of Wrath (1940), and that the award was probably 'deferred payment for his work on Mr. Smith Goes To Washington (1939)'.

CONTINUED

Interesting Facts

Cary Grant demanded top billing and $100,000 salary, a huge amount at the time. As it turned out, however, he donated his entire earnings to the British War Relief Fund.

Katharine Hepburn starred in the Broadway production of the play on which this film was based and owned the film rights to the material; they were purchased for her by billionaire Howard Hughes, then given to her as a gift.

James Stewart wasn't at all comfortable with some of the dialog, especially in the swimming pool scene, which also required him to act in a dressing gown. He said at the time that if he'd played the scene in just a swimming costume it would have been the end of his career.

Quotes

C. K. Dexter Haven: Sometimes, for your own sake, Red, I think you should've stuck to me longer.
Tracy Lord: I thought it was for life, but the nice judge gave me a full pardon.
C. K. Dexter Haven: Aaah, that's the old redhead. No bitterness, no recrimination, just a good swift left to the jaw.

Macaulay Connor: Oh Tracy darling...
Tracy Lord: Mike...
Macaulay Connor: What can I say to you? Tell me darling.
Tracy Lord: Not anything - don't say anything. And especially not 'darling'.

Tracy Lord: The time to make up your mind about people is never.

THE GRAPES OF WRATH

Directed by: John Ford - Runtime: 2 hours 9 minutes

After their drought-ridden farm is seized by the bank the Joad family, led by just-paroled son Tom, loads up a truck and heads West. On the road, beset by hardships, the Joads meet dozens of other families making the same trek and holding onto the same dream. Once in California, however, the Joads soon realise that the promised land isn't quite what they hoped.

STARRING

Henry Fonda
Born: 16th May 1905
Died: 12th August 1982

Character:
Tom Joad

Film and stage actor, Fonda made his Hollywood debut in 1935 and his career gained momentum after his Academy Award-nominated performance as Tom Joad in The Grapes Of Wrath. Throughout six decades in Hollywood he cultivated a strong appealing screen image and won an Academy Award for Best Actor for his final film role in the movie On Golden Pond (1981). In 1999, he was named the sixth-Greatest Male Star of All Time by the American Film Institute.

Jane Darwell
Born: 15th October 1879
Died: 13th August 1967

Characters:
Ma Joad

Actress of stage, film and television who appeared in more than one hundred major motion pictures spanning half a century. She is perhaps best-remembered for her poignant portrayal of the matriarch and leader of the Joad family in John Steinbeck's The Grapes Of Wrath, for which she received the Academy Award for Best Supporting Actress. In 1960 Darwell received a star on the Hollywood Walk of Fame for her contributions to the motion-picture industry.

John Carradine
Born: 5th February 1906
Died: 27th November 1988

Character:
Jim Casy

Actor, best known for his roles in horror films, Westerns and Shakespearean theatre. A member of Cecil B. DeMille's stock company and later John Ford's company, he was one of the most prolific character actors in Hollywood history and starred in over 230 films throughout his career. For his contributions to the film industry Carradine was inducted into the Hollywood Walk of Fame in 1960, and the Western Performers Hall of Fame in 2003.

TRIVIA

Goofs	One of the cars (number plate 263 with the silver bed springs sticking out of the back) evacuating the Department of Agriculture camp site leaves the camp twice, once before the Joads pack up and once after.
	When the Joads set out from the petrol station to cross the desert you see them pull away from the station twice.
Interesting Facts	Writer John Steinbeck loved the film and said that Henry Fonda as Tom Joad made him believe his own words.

Interesting Facts

Prior to filming producer Darryl F. Zanuck sent undercover investigators out to the migrant camps to see if John Steinbeck had been exaggerating about the squalor and unfair treatment meted out there. He was horrified to discover that, if anything, Steinbeck had actually downplayed what went on in the camps.

Director John Ford banned all makeup and perfume from the set on the grounds that it was not in keeping with the tone of the picture.

Henry Fonda kept the hat he wore in the movie for the rest of his life, until before he passed away in 1982 when he gave it to his old friend Jane Withers. Apparently, he and Withers, when she was an 8-year-old girl and he a young man, did a play together before Fonda made it in film. Fonda was so nervous to go onstage that little Jane took his hand, said a little prayer to ease his nerves, and the two of them became good friends for life.

Although John Carradine hated John Ford's bullying style of direction he nevertheless made eleven films with him over a period of 28 years. Ford was particularly keen on Carradine's unusual look.

Quote

[last lines]
Ma Joad: Rich fellas come up an' they die, an' their kids ain't no good an' they die out. But we keep a'comin'. We're the people that live. They can't wipe us out; they can't lick us. We'll go on forever, Pa, 'cause we're the people.

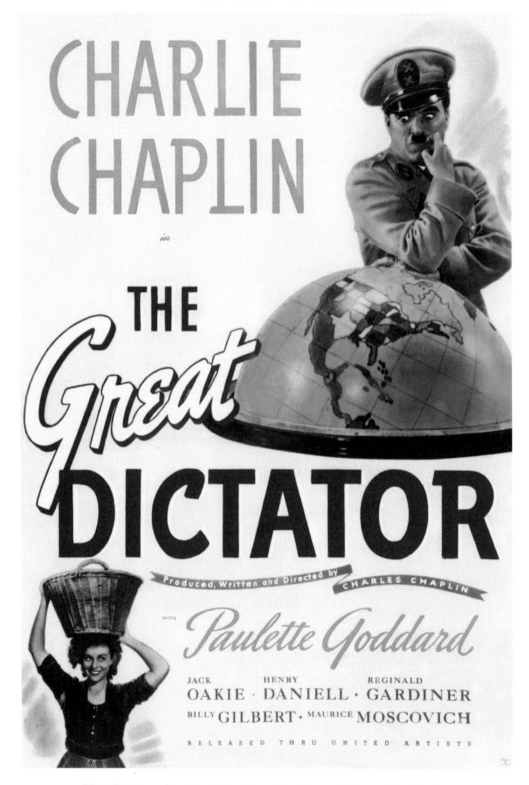

Directed by: Charles Chaplin - Runtime: 2 hours 5 minutes

Dictator Adenoid Hynkel tries to expand his empire while a poor Jewish barber tries to avoid persecution from Hynkel's regime.

STARRING

Charlie Chaplin
Born: 16th April 1889
Died: 25th December 1977

Character:
Hynkel - Dictator of
Tomania / A Jewish Barber

Sir Charles Spencer 'Charlie' Chaplin was an English comic actor, filmmaker and composer who rose to fame in the silent era. Chaplin became a worldwide icon through his screen persona 'the Tramp' and is considered one of the most important figures in the history of the film industry. His career spanned more than 75 years from his childhood in Victorian England until a year before his death in 1977.

Paulette Goddard
Born: 3rd June 1910
Died: 23rd April 1990

Character:
Hannah

Goddard was a child fashion model and performer in several Broadway productions as a Ziegfeld Girl. She became a major star for Paramount Studios in the 1940s and her most notable films were as Charles Chaplin's leading lady in Modern Times (her first major role) and his subsequent film The Great Dictator. She was nominated for an Academy Award for Best Supporting Actress for her performance in So Proudly We Hail! (1943).

Jack Oakie
Born: 12th November 1903
Died: 23rd January 1978

Character:
Napaloni - Dictator of
Bacteria

Actor, starring mostly in films but also on stage, radio and television. Oakie worked in various musicals and comedies on Broadway from 1923 to 1927, before leaving to go to Hollywood to work in movies. He signed with Paramount Pictures in 1927 and made his first talking film, The Dummy, in 1929. His portrayal of Napaloni in The Great Dictator earned him a nomination for the Academy Award for Best Supporting Actor.

TRIVIA

Goofs When the Barber and Schultz are flying upside down, the wire waving Schultz's scarf can be seen.

When the barber slides into the basement window while evading the stormtrooper, his hat falls off onto the street. In the next shot he is wearing his hat again.

Interesting Facts According to documentaries on the making of the film, Charles Chaplin began to feel more uncomfortable lampooning Adolf Hitler the more he heard of Hitler's actions in Europe. Ultimately, the invasion of France inspired Chaplin to change the ending of his film to include his famous speech.

Interesting Facts

Adolf Hitler banned the film in Germany and in all countries occupied by the Nazis. Curiosity got the best of him though and he had a print brought in through Portugal. History records that he screened it twice, in private, but history did not record his reaction to the film. Chaplin said, "I'd give anything to know what he thought of it." For political reasons in Germany the ban stayed in place after the end of WWII and until 1958.

The film was released eleven years after the end of the silent era and was Chaplin's first all-talking, all-sound film. It was financed entirely by Chaplin and was his biggest box-office hit.

The German spoken by the dictator is complete nonsense and was improvised. The language in which the shop signs, posters, etc in the Jewish quarter are written is Esperanto, a language created in 1887 by Dr L.L. Zamenhof, a Polish Jew.

Quotes

Schultz: Strange, and I always thought of you as an Aryan.
A Jewish Barber: I'm a vegetarian

Madame Napaloni: *[arriving at the Tomainia train station]* Papa, why can't-a we get out here?
Napaloni - Dictator of Bacteria: There is-a no carpet.
Madame Napaloni: Who cares about a carpet?
Napaloni - Dictator of Bacteria: Il Digaditchi, me, a-Napaloni, I never get out without a carpet!

Adenoid Hynkel: Ah, de Aryan. Und de Aryan maiden. Ah, de Aryan maiden! Ah, the delicatessen bitte schön.

PINOCCHIO

Directors: Ben Sharpsteen / Hamilton Luske - Runtime: 1 hour 28 minutes

A living puppet, with the help of a cricket as his conscience, must prove himself worthy to become a real boy.

TRIVIA

Goofs | Pinocchio and Lampwick are seen hanging out together playing eight ball pool, but eight ball pool didn't exist until around 1908 and this film is presumably set in the 19th century.

When Pinocchio plays with the candle he burns his left hand but Gepetto puts Pinocchio's right hand into the water.

Interesting Facts | Walt Disney insisted that the identities of all the actors and singers providing the voices for his characters were kept secret. He believed that if audiences knew who was providing the voice that the magic would be ruined.

Figaro the cat was Walt Disney's favourite character. Disney pushed for the kitten to appear in the film as much as possible.

Originally budgeted at $500,000, the development of the film caused it to go way over budget and ultimately cost $2.5 million, one of the most expensive films ever produced at the time.

The theme song from Pinocchio, "When You Wish Upon A Star", was ranked No.7 in the 2004 American Film Institute's List of the Top Movie Songs of All Time, the highest-ranking song on the list among Disney animated films.

Pinocchio was the first animated film to win an Academy Award in a competitive category; Snow White And The Seven Dwarfs (1937) had won a Special Academy Award two years earlier.

Quotes | **The Blue Fairy:** A lie keeps growing and growing until it's as plain as the nose on your face.

Jiminy Cricket: You buttered your bread. Now sleep in it!

The Blue Fairy: Prove yourself brave, truthful, and unselfish, and someday, you will be a real boy.

SPORTING WINNERS

FOOTBALL

England: The abandoned 1939-1940 season would have been the 48th season of the Football League. It began on Saturday 26th August 1939 but all play ended after just three games due to the British declaration of war on Germany on the 3rd September. At the time it was abandoned Blackpool were leading the First Division with 6 points.

Scotland: The 1939-1940 season would have been the 50th season of Scottish Football League. It was suspended on the 3rd September 1939 after five rounds of games played in Division One and four rounds in Division Two. At that time of its suspension Rangers were leading the First Division with 9 points followed by Falkirk with 8 points.

FOOTBALL LEAGUE WAR CUP FINAL

West Ham United	1-0	Blackburn Rovers
Small ⚽ 34'		

Attendance: 42,300

The 1940 Football League War Cup Final was contested by West Ham United and Blackburn Rovers. It was played on the 8th June 1940 and kicked off at 6.30pm, despite fears that London would be bombed by the Luftwaffe. The wartime crowd included wounded members of the BEF recently evacuated from Dunkirk. West Ham won the tie 1-0 and the trophy was presented to the winning team by A. V. Alexander, First Lord of the Admiralty.

As the match was played during wartime no reception was held for the winning team. Some of the players went to the Boleyn public house on Green Street for a few pints whilst others returned immediately to their service units.

Rugby - Home Nations

The 1940 Home Nations Championship series was another competition not contested due to the outbreak of World War II in September 1939. International rugby had been put on hold and would not resume again until 1947 when the Home Nations Championship became the Five Nation Championship (with the addition of France to the line-up).

Grand National - Bogskar

The start of the 1940 Grand National; *the winner Bogskar (No.20) is pictured on the left.*

The 1940 Grand National was the 99th renewal of this world-famous horse race and took place at Aintree Racecourse near Liverpool on the 5th April. The race was contested by 30 horses and was won by Bogskar, a 25/1 shot trained and owned by Lord Stalbridge, and ridden by Royal Air Force sergeant Mervyn Jones. This was the last true Aintree Grand National before a five-year break due to World War II.

Pos.	Name	Jockey	Age	Weight	Odds
1st	**Bogskar**	**Mervyn Jones**	7	**10st 4lb**	25/1
2nd	MacMoffat	Ian Alder	8	10st 10lb	
3rd	Gold Arrow	Peter Lay	8	10st 3lb	
4th	Symaethis	Matthew Feakes	8	10st 7 lb	

Epsom Derby - Pont L'Eveque

Winner.	Jockey	Trainer	Owner	Winning Margin	Time
Pont l'Eveque	**Sam Wragg**	**Fred Darling**	**Fred Darling**	**3 lengths**	**2m 30.8s**

The Derby Stakes is Britain's richest horse race and the most prestigious of the country's five Classics. First run in 1780 this Group 1 flat horse race is open to three year old thoroughbred colts and fillies. Although the race usually takes place at Epsom Downs in Surrey, during both World Wars the venue was changed and the Derby was run at Newmarket; these races are known as the New Derby.

GOLF - OPEN CHAMPIONSHIP

Originally scheduled to be played at Birkdale Golf Club, Merseyside, the 1940 Open Championship was cancelled due to the war and the tournament was not contested again until 1946. Birkdale Golf Club eventually did manage to host the Open Championship but had to wait until 1954 to do so.

TENNIS - WIMBLEDON

The 1940 Wimbledon Championships, the world's oldest tennis tournament, was another sporting event cancelled due to the outbreak of World War 2. Hosted since 1877 by the All England Lawn Tennis and Croquet Club in Wimbledon, London, the competition would not resume again until 1946.

COUNTY CRICKET

All first-class cricket was cancelled in the 1940 to 1944 English cricket seasons because of the Second World War; no first-class matches were played in England after Friday, 1st September 1939 until Saturday, 19th May 1945.

WORLD SNOOKER CHAMPIONSHIP - JOE DAVIS

Joe Davis ✚ 37 - 36 ✚ Fred Davis

The 1940 World Snooker Championship was held at Thurston's Hall in London between the 22nd February and 20th March. Joe Davis won his fourteenth World title by defeating his younger brother Fred Davis in the final. This was the last World Championship to be held until the end of the Second World War.

THE COST OF LIVING

MINISTRY OF FOOD

REASONS FOR RATIONING

War has meant the re-planning of our food supplies. Half our meat and most of our bacon, butter and sugar come from overseas. Here are four reasons for rationing:—

1 **RATIONING PREVENTS WASTE OF FOOD** We must not ask our sailors to bring us unnecessary food cargoes at the risk of their lives.

2 **RATIONING INCREASES OUR WAR EFFORT** Our shipping carries food, and armaments in their raw and finished state, and other essential raw materials for home consumption and the export trade. To reduce our purchases of food abroad is to release ships for bringing us other imports. So we shall strengthen our war effort.

3 **RATIONING DIVIDES SUPPLIES EQUALLY** There will be ample supplies for our 44½ million people, but we must divide them fairly, everyone being treated alike. No one must be left out.

4 **RATIONING PREVENTS UNCERTAINTY** Your Ration Book assures you of your fair share. Rationing means that there will be no uncertainty—*and no queues.*

YOUR RATION BOOK IS YOUR PASSPORT TO EASY PURCHASING OF BACON & HAM, BUTTER AND SUGAR

AN ANNOUNCEMENT BY THE MINISTRY OF FOOD, GT. WESTMINSTER HOUSE, LONDON, S.W.I

COMPARISON CHART

	1940	1940 + Inflation	2019	% Change
3 Bedroom House	£700	£44,908	£236,676	+427%
Weekly Income	£2.8s.5d	£155.31	£569	+266.4%
Pint Of Beer	9d	£2.41	£3.69	+53.1%
Cheese (lb)	1s.5d	£4.54	£3.09	-31.2%
Bacon (lb)	1s.9d	£5.61	£2.65	-52.8%
The Beano	2d	53p	£2.75	+418.9%

SHOPPING

Bournville Cocoa (quarter lb)	5d
Rowntree's Cocoa (½lb)	9½d
Batchelor's Peas (medium can)	7d
Foster Clark's Soups (2 servings)	1d
Coleman's Vitacup	6d
Symington's Table Creams (packet)	4½d
Kellogg's Corn Flakes (family packet)	5d
Quick Quaker Oats (40 servings)	8½d
Huntley & Palmers Golden Bix (½lb)	6d
Rowntrees Dairy Box (½lb box)	1s.1d
Black Magic Chocolates (1lb box)	2s.10d
Bassett's Liquorice Allsorts (carton)	2d
Smarties (tube)	2d
Rowntree's Fruit Gums (tube)	2d
Eve Shampoo	2½d
Amami Luxury Shampoo	3d
Sta-Set Quick Wave Set (tablet)	6d
Arrid Cream Deodorant (jar)	6d
Vaseline Petroleum Jelly (jar)	4½d
Macleans Peroxide Tooth Paste	6d
Phillips' Dental Magnesia	6d
Glymiel Jelly (tube)	6d
Andrews Liver Salts (tin)	9d
Beechams Lung Syrup	1s.3d
Ex-Lax	2d
Aspro	3d
Sylvan Flakes (giant pack)	1s
Winalot Wholemeal Dog Food (packet)	5d
Spillers Shapes Dog Food (packet)	5d

CLOTHES

Women's Clothing

Blue Fox-Dyed Lamb Fur Coat	15gns
Burberry Warm Fleece Topcoat	£7.10s
C&A Hooded Coat	£1.7s.6d
Burberry Pure Felt Hat	15s.6d
C&A All Wool Pleated Skirt	12s.11d
Portland Comfort Shoes	£1.2s.6d

Men's Clothing

Burberry Tweed Overcoat	£5
Cheviot Tweed Lounge Suit	£5.10s
Vantella Shirt	10s.6d

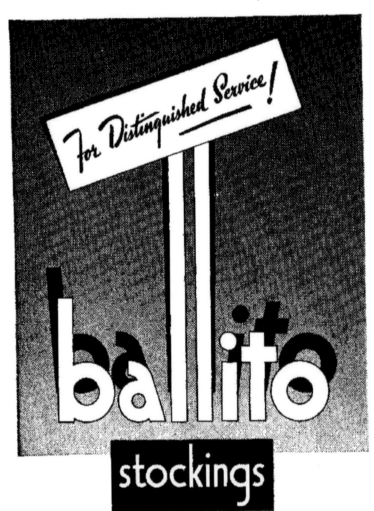

OTHER PRICES

Hillman Minx Car	£165
Riley Twelve Car	£310
Wolseley Ten Series Car	£237
Hercules Bicycle	£4.19s.9d
Kropp Razor (black handle)	10s.6d
Buckfast Tonic Wine (large bottle)	7s.6d
Stones Orange Tonic Wine	3s.3d
K4 Cigarettes (10)	6d
Black Cat Cigarettes (10)	6d
Radio Times Magazine	2d

2 hours' steady nourishment for 2d

Kit Kat CHOCOLATE CRISP
MADE ONLY BY ROWNTREE'S

FOUR big wafer biscuits, oven-crisp and crunchy, a lacing of finest butter and creamy milk chocolate in between, *and* a thick coating of milk chocolate all round! Isn't that the most amazing 2d. worth you ever heard of? And, you know, this particular type of chocolate block produces a *slower* rise of blood-sugar, which gives you longer endurance and staying power. That's why we call Chocolate Crisp the biggest little meal in Britain. It gives you energy to make a *good* job of whatever you're doing.

THE BIGGEST LITTLE MEAL IN BRITAIN! 2d

MONEY CONVERSION TABLE

Old Money		Equivalent
Farthing	¼d	0.1p
Half Penny	½d	0.21p
Penny	1d	0.42p
Threepence	3d	1.25p
Sixpence	6d	2.5p
Shilling	1s	5p
Florin	2s	10p
Half Crown	2s.6d	12.5p
Crown	5s	25p
Ten Shillings	10s	50p
Pound	20s	£1
Guinea	21s	£1.05

CARTOONS

Useless Eustace

"What! My turn for leave? Aw, gee! Sarge. What have I done wrong now?"

Useless Eustace

"Blimey! It looks as though I've got a rotten billet, Nobby!—the old girl says she's going to treat me like one of the family!"

Useless Eustace

"What d'you mean, 'friend'? You know darn well you hate the ruddy sight of me!"

JANE . . .

ARE YOU SURE IT'S KISSPROOF?

YOU LOOK VERY DETERMINED, MY DEAR!

YES, I MEAN TO DO MY BIT, TOO, COLONEL!

— I'M GOING TO KISS THE WHOLE BATTALION. GOODBYE!

JANE . . .

WHY DO YOU CONTINUALLY TRAVEL TO HOLLAND AND BACK, PROFESSOR WRYNECK?

RESEARCH, COMMANDER!— I AM A HUMBLE STUDENT OF ORNITHOLOGY!

MAX!—INTERPRETER WANTED!

THIS GENTLEMAN MAY BE BRITISH — BUT HE'S SPEAKING DOUBLE-DUTCH!

Printed in Great Britain
by Amazon